# RACE CAR LEGENDS

*The Allisons*
*Mario Andretti*
*Jeff Burton*
*Crashes & Collisions*
*Demolition Derby*
*Drag Racing*
*Dale Earnhardt*
*Famous Finishes*
*Formula One Racing*
*A. J. Foyt*
*Jeff Gordon*
*The History of NASCAR*
*Indy Car Racing*
*Kenny Irwin Jr.*
*The Jarretts*
*The Labonte Brothers*
*Lowriders*
*The Making of a Race Car*
*Mark Martin*
*Jeremy Mayfield*
*Monster Trucks & Tractors*
*Motorcycles*
*The Need for Speed*
*Off-Road Racing*
*Richard Petty*
*The Pit Crew*
*Tony Stewart*
*Stunt Driving*
*The Unsers*
*Rusty Wallace*
*Women in Racing*

## CHELSEA HOUSE PUBLISHERS

RACE CAR LEGENDS

# INDY CAR RACING

*Bruce and Becky Durost Fish*

CHELSEA HOUSE PUBLISHERS
Philadelphia

Frontis: *Indy cars speed around the track at the 1996 Indianapolis 500. That year the race's prize money was a record-setting $8.1 million—quite an increase over the $25,000 offered at the first Indy 500 in 1911.*

Produced by
21st Century Publishing and Communications, Inc.
New York, New York
http://www.21cpc.com

CHELSEA HOUSE PUBLISHERS

Production Manager: Pamela Loos
Art Director: Sara Davis
Director of Photography: Judy L. Hasday
Managing Editor: James D. Gallagher
Senior Production Editor: J. Christopher Higgins
Publishing Coordinator/Project Editor: James McAvoy
Editorial Assistant: Rob Quinn

The Chelsea House World Wide Web address is
http://www.chelseahouse.com

First Printing

1 3 5 7 9 8 6 4 2

Library of Congress Cataloging-in-Publication Data

Fish, Bruce.
   Indy car racing / Bruce and Becky Durost Fish.
       p.    cm.—(Race car legends)
   Includes bibliographical references and index.
   ISBN 0-7910-5845-X
   1. Indianapolis Speedway Race—History—Juvenile literature. [ 1. Indianapolis Speedway Race. 2. Automobile racing.] I. Fish, Becky Durost. II. Title. III. Series.

GV1033.5.I55 F57 2000
796.72'09772'52—dc21

                                                                00-031467
                                                                        CIP
                                                                        AC

# CONTENTS

CHAPTER 1
CARL FISHER'S DREAM  7

CHAPTER 2
ANOTHER VICTORY FOR EDDIE  17

CHAPTER 3
TONY HULMAN'S REVOLUTION  27

CHAPTER 4
THE GREATEST SPECTACLE
IN RACING  35

CHAPTER 5
A DECADE OF CHALLENGES  45

CHAPTER 6
THE FIGHT TO CONTROL INDY  53

GLOSSARY  60
CHRONOLOGY  61
FURTHER READING  63
INDEX  64

# CARL FISHER'S DREAM

When Ray Harroun drove his Marmon Wasp race car across the finish line of the first Indy 500 in 1911, he wasn't trying to make history. He was just trying to win a little-known race in a small Midwestern city.

A man named Carl Fisher was determined that the race wouldn't remain obscure for long. Fisher had big plans for automobile racing in America. And he wanted the most important races to be held in Indianapolis, Indiana.

Carl Fisher was a dreamer who fell in love with anything fast. His family had moved to Indianapolis in 1886, when he was 12 years old. He got caught up in the bicycle craze sweeping the country. Riding on a mechanical device that could go as fast as a horse was exciting. Not too long after that, Fisher quit school and went to work repairing bicycles.

By the late 1890s, Carl Fisher discovered a new way to go fast—the automobile. In 1900, he became a dealer for Oldsmobile. He established a company, the Fisher Auto Company, which became the foundation for his future business and real estate empire.

Fisher never outgrew his love of speed. He decided

*Ray Harroun makes history as the winner of the first Indianapolis 500 in 1911. His Marmon Wasp averaged almost 75 mph—an amazing feat at the time.*

that American automakers needed a racetrack where they could test their designs against each other. He wanted a track that was larger, safer, and faster than anything previously built. He imagined such a speedway could also host motorcycle and airplane demonstrations.

On December 12, 1908, Carl Fisher paid $72,000 for 320 acres of land, a property located a few miles northwest of downtown Indianapolis. Both a railroad line and a trolley line ran right by it, making it easy for people to get to.

Three longtime business associates joined Fisher in his project: Jim Allison, Arthur C. Newby, and Frank H. Wheeler. In less then two months, the Indianapolis Motor Speedway Corporation (IMS) was created, backed by $250,000 from the four investors. They planned to hold a series of races every month throughout that spring and summer.

Engineer P. T. Andrews was brought in from New York to design and construct the Speedway. It featured four turns, each a quarter-mile long. Two five-eighth-mile straightaways ran along the east and west sides. On the north and south were two one-eighth-mile legs or chutes. Straight sections of the track were 50 feet wide, spreading out to 60 feet wide on the turns. The total distance of the oval was two-and-a-half miles. Plenty of room remained for grandstands to hold the huge crowds Fisher expected.

Starting in March 1909, hundreds of workers began erecting more than 40 buildings and laying out the track. The surface of the track was made from a mixture of tar, gravel, limestone, and stone dust rolled onto a firm layer of clay.

On Monday, August 17, 1909, practice sessions for the first auto race began. Driving on the

track in hot weather caused oil to work its way down through the surface, loosening pieces of gravel and dust. By Wednesday afternoon, the track began to break up. Practice sessions were stopped, and repairs began.

The track wasn't ready until Thursday morning, when the gates opened for the first day of races. As the morning races ended, the track began to break up again. During the 250-mile Prest-O-Lite trophy race that afternoon, driver William Bourque's car hit a pothole on the main straightaway. It spun out of control, hit a ditch, and flipped over. Both Bourque and his mechanic, who was also in the car, were killed. When the three-day racing event was over, five people were dead.

Despite the tragedies, Fisher and his partners proclaimed success. That weekend, the Speedway drew 75,000 spectators. But something

*Carl Fisher found an outlet for his love of speed as a dealer in Oldsmobiles, like the early model pictured here.*

had to be done about the track's surface. The American Automobile Association (AAA), which set the rules and standards for auto racing in the United States, seemed ready to declare the Indianapolis Motor Speedway unfit for future races.

The IMS canceled September events. P. T. Andrews tested different materials to see which would provide the safest, fastest, and most durable surface for racing. Brick won out, but it was much more expensive than concrete. Carl Fisher didn't care. He wanted the best, no matter what it cost. IMS would be the first racetrack in the world made from brick.

A small army of bricklayers set 3.2 million paving bricks. The outer edges of the four corners were lined with three-foot-high concrete retaining walls to keep cars from sliding into the crowds. The job was finished in 63 days. People began to call the IMS "the Brickyard." Its investors had now spent $680,000.

During 1910, IMS was the site of many races. Later that year, Fisher and his partners discussed the ideal distance for a world-class race to be held the next May. They settled on 500 miles because it allowed them to test both drivers and cars, while still having time to get large crowds in and out of the facility during daylight hours. To make their Memorial Day event unique, they offered $25,000 in total prize money, roughly 10 times the amount normally paid for a day of racing.

The first Indy 500 was held on May 30, 1911, before a crowd of 80,000. Unlike today's racing cars, these cars held two people. One was the driver, and the other was a mechanic. Mechanics were important. Cars didn't have mirrors, so the mechanics told their drivers when other cars were coming up from behind. They helped solve mechanical problems, and if their car stalled, they jumped out, ran around the front, and used the hand crank to get it started again.

Ray Harroun stunned everyone when he showed up without a mechanic. He had removed the second seat from his Marmon Wasp to make it lighter. There was talk of disqualifying Harroun's car as unsafe. But he pointed out the mirror he had mounted on the hood of his car. He would use it to see cars in back of him. Many people believe that Harroun's car was the first to use a rearview mirror.

Making his car lighter wasn't the only thing Harroun did to give himself an advantage in the race. During qualifying runs, he watched drivers damage their tires by going too fast. They then had to change their tires during pit stops, which gave other drivers chances to catch up with or even pass them. Harroun calculated that he would get better wear from his tires if he kept his speed down to 75 miles per hour (mph), eliminating several pit stops. He was positive that the time he saved would give him the chance to win the race. His strategy worked. Harroun won the first Indy 500 in 7 hours and 42 minutes.

Harroun's victory was almost as much a physical triumph as a mechanical one. Driving early race cars was a dirty, exhausting, and dangerous job. The race cars were usually stripped-down passenger cars. Narrow, hard tires, and the simple suspensions transferred every bump in the road directly to the thinly padded bucket seats, pounding the drivers' bodies. The ride was also deafening because mufflers weren't attached to the large exhaust pipes, in order to get maximum power from the engines.

The cars were hard to steer, and shifting gears was even more difficult. By the end of a race, many drivers had bloody hands. Without seat belts to hold them in place, they braced themselves with their feet and arms. The cars did not have doors or windshields, either. Dust, cold air, rocks, oil, and other debris pummeled the drivers. Goggles and leather helmets offered little protection.

Only the rear wheels had brakes, making them nearly useless during a race. Though the workmanship of the cars was quite good, the engines burned gallons of oil and gasoline. Great clouds of oily blue smoke often created bad visibility on the track. The engines also leaked oil onto the track, making it slippery. During the first 500 miles of an Indy race, the best-built cars leaked about 12 gallons of oil. One car used 104 gallons.

In spite of these discomforts, racing became popular. In 1912, Carl Fisher added to its attractions. He increased the total prize money at Indy to more than $50,000, making it the highest paying sporting event in the world. The winner would receive $50,000 at a time when skilled factory workers made only $2.50 a day.

That year, the AAA changed the rules, limiting the number of cars allowed on closed race tracks. Indy could accept only 33 competitors.

Near the end of the 1912 race, Ralph DePalma appeared to be on his way to victory. Then his Mercedes broke down and came to a stop 1.5 laps from the finish. DePalma and his mechanic became instant heroes when they pushed their car all the way back to the pit area. They were greeted by a cheering crowd.

A promotional overseas trip in late 1913

attracted interest in Indy from European automakers. These teams brought new ideas about
car design. Peugeot's car featured an engine that
used two overhead camshafts to open and close
the valves. The top of each combustion chamber
had a rounded top. These changes produced
greater power and reliability. The car also had
lightweight wire wheels that could be removed
quickly by unscrewing a single nut in the center
of the hub. All four wheels had brakes.

The Peugeot was driven by Frenchman Jules
Goux. Goux hired American driver Johnny Aitken
to advise him on tactics. Aitken looked at the 90-
degree temperatures and made one suggestion:
slow down, and save your car. Heat could spell big
trouble for both engines and tires.

Once the race began, most of the fastest drivers were quickly locked into a battle for first
place. Goux stayed farther back, fighting the
desire to show off his car's power. As the miles

*Race cars at the starting line, around 1920. By the early 1920s, designers had begun building cars specifically for racing, improving weight, speed, and performance.*

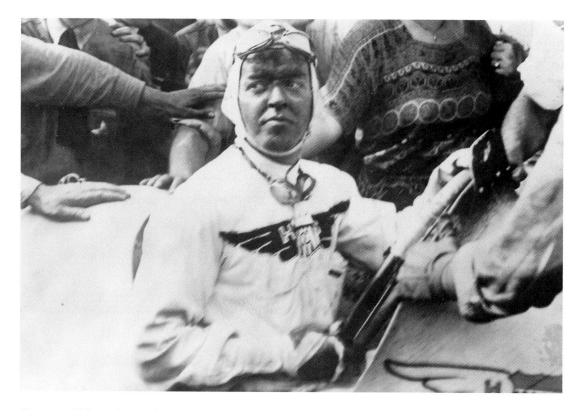

*Tommy Milton (above) won the 1923 Indy 500 in his single-seat racing car. He was the first driver to win the race twice.*

rolled by, many leaders dropped out with engine problems. Those who remained were forced to make repeated pit stops for new tires. Finally, Goux was given the signal by his crew—push the car's limits. He worked his way toward the front of the field. Then he cruised to victory at an average of 75.933 mph.

The 1915 race was the first in which cars were lined up according to their qualifying speed. The fastest car was given the inside position on the first row, closest to the pole that marked the start/finish line. It became known as the pole position.

The European presence grew in both 1914 and 1915 but was absent from 1916 to 1918 because of World War I. However, advances in building airplanes for the war were carried over to racing cars after the war. By 1922 some cars were specifically designed for racing. Aerodynamic features such as smooth sides and a pointed tail were standard. Engines were smaller and more efficient. Most cars used lightweight aluminum in both the body and engine. Four-wheel hydraulic brake systems and better tires resulted in better performance and a much smoother ride. The engines leaked less oil.

At the 1923 Indy, Tommy Milton became the first driver to win for a second time. This was also the year that made single-seat racing cars standard at Indy. Onboard mechanics were no longer needed because the cars were much more reliable—and they didn't need to be started with a hand crank.

Automaker Fred Duesenberg brought the first supercharger to Indy in 1924. His main competitor, Harry Miller, answered with a front-wheel drive, supercharged car in 1925. While Miller came in second to the Duesenberg driven by Peter DePaolo, his car set the standard for the rest of the decade. DePaolo became famous for being the first driver to win the Indy 500 with an average speed of more than 100 mph. He chose a good race to win. For the first time, radio broadcasts of the race reached most of the country.

Carl Fisher's dream of creating the world's best racetrack was fulfilled. However, changes were on the way for the IMS, and Fisher would not be part of them.

# ANOTHER VICTORY FOR EDDIE

In 1927, new ownership took over the Indianapolis Motor Speedway. Backed by a group of investors from Detroit, Eddie Rickenbacker bought out Carl Fisher and his partners for $700,000 and became the president of the Speedway.

Rickenbacker was a household name in America at the time. In 1903, when his father died, 13-year-old Eddie left school to support his family. He did odd jobs for two years and earned a mail-order degree in mechanical engineering. At age 15, he became a mechanic. The job paid 75¢ a day. In the second decade of the 1900s, Eddie drove racing cars, and eventually created his own four-car team.

When the United States entered World War I in 1917, 27-year-old Eddie joined the army. He soon convinced his commanding officer to send him to flight school. Eddie was assigned to the famous 94th Aero Pursuit "Hat in the Ring" Squadron. In less than seven months, he shot down 22 German planes. His success earned him the title "Ace of Aces."

*Eddie Rickenbacker, a World War I flying ace, poses with his airplane. After the war, Rickenbacker bought the Indianapolis Motor Speedway and made many changes to Indy racing, which boosted the popularity of the sport.*

Because of this fame, after the war people offered Eddie important jobs connected with his love of cars and planes. He made a good living, but he never forgot what it was like to try to support a family on a small salary.

That memory was one reason he decided some of the rules at Indy needed to be changed. Racing fans wanted to get good value for their money. Eddie Rickenbacker saw three problems that might eventually drive fans away.

First, the 91.5-cubic-inch limit placed on engine size in 1926 had been too successful. As intended, it kept car speeds down. But Peter DePaolo's 1925 average speed record of 101.13 mph still stood. Fans wanted to see records broken. They wanted cars to be driven faster and faster. Unless the rules allowed larger engines, no one would exceed the record DePaolo had coaxed from his 122-cubic-inch Duesenberg engine. The Indy 500 would get boring, and fewer paying customers would show up.

The second problem was that just about all the teams were using either Miller or Duesenberg-style cars. The Miller 91 was used by 8 of the top 10 finishers at Indy in both 1927 and 1928. Rickenbacker sensed that fans wanted to see more variety in the cars competing. Unless engines were allowed to be bigger, passenger-car companies such as General Motors, Chrysler, and Ford wouldn't enter the race.

A third problem Eddie Rickenbacker saw was the extremely high cost of racing. The Miller 91 cost $15,000. A racing team then spent about $10,000 for two replacement engines. Another $10,000 went for various hand-finished pieces used in the car. By the time the additional costs to transport the car and team to the race, buy

the fuel, and pay the crew were added, a top team easily spent $50,000 during the month of May. All this money was needed to run in only one race. Most people sitting in the stands drove cars that cost less than $1,000. How could the average person relate to cars that cost so much more than the car they drove to the racetrack?

The Contest Board of Indy drew up new rules for the 1930 season. These rules essentially outlawed the exotic cars and encouraged teams

*During the 1930s, Indy cars like this 1932 Chevrolet were required to weigh at least 1,750 pounds and have two seats—one for the driver and one for the mechanic.*

*The Indianapolis Motor Speedway (pictured here in the 1990s) has undergone many renovations over the years. What began as a brick track is now one of the safest and most modern raceways in the world.*

to use modified passenger cars. Engines could be as large as 366 cubic inches. Each car had to weigh at least 1,750 pounds and include two seats. These changes cut the cost of building a race car from $15,000 to $1,500.

At first, racers called the new rules the "Junk Formula." But as America entered the Great Depression and money became hard to find, they were grateful that racing at Indy had become less expensive.

The Junk Formula gave racing teams all kinds of options for building a car. Because cars used before 1922 weighed 1,763 pounds and had two seats, some teams dragged out their old cars from storage and put new engines in them. Other teams kept their Duesenberg or Miller engines, widened the body of the car so that it would hold two seats, then added some weight to bring the car up to the new minimum. Some teams tried to get more power by using two small racing engines in one car.

Still other teams used passenger-car engines from Studebaker, Hudson, Buick, Stutz, Chrysler, and Ford. These flathead engines could be "hot-rodded" cheaply by milling the head to increase compression and using better pistons and valves. These engines also used more carbure- tors, a cam with more overlap, exhaust headers, and a lighter flywheel. None of these changes were great secrets, and they are still used by both amateurs and professionals today.

Racers also came up with new engine ideas. Back in 1926, Harry Miller had designed an engine for boat racing. A driver adapted the engine for dirt-track racing. After the Indy rules changed, the Miller engine was used at Indy. A car powered by that engine finished second in the 1930 race.

The next year, Harry Miller decided to develop another simple, reliable racing engine that could be used both on dirt tracks and at Indy. He wanted it to sell for only $2,000. Working with Leo Goossen, Miller designed a four-cylinder engine. He did the tooling for it. Then he ran out of money.

Fred Offenhauser bought the rights to Miller's engine. With the assistance of Louie Meyer,

Offenhauser used the engine as the foundation for the Offenhauser Engineering Company. The engine came to be known as the Offy. It was available in two sizes and reached 5,500 revolutions per minute (rpm). The engine weighed just 385 pounds and cost $2,000. Any car mechanic could work on it. The Offy went on to win dozens of Indy 500 races and became the standard engine to use at Indy.

Eventually Offenhauser sold his business to Dale Drake and Louie Meyer. Meyer started out as a mechanic. At the 1927 Indy, he drove 41 laps as a relief driver and decided that he wanted to switch to driving race cars. The next year he won Indy, and he finished second in 1929 after stalling in the pits. In 1933, he won his second Indy. Three years later, he became the first driver to win three Indy 500s. He toasted his victory with milk, a tradition that has been followed ever since.

The improvements people like Meyer and Miller made in engines, combined with the 1930 rule changes, increased average speeds at Indy. In 1930, the winning car averaged 100.448 mph, a significant increase at these rates of speed for the time. By 1935, that average had increased again to 106.240 mph.

Before another jump in average speed could happen, though, the Brickyard needed major renovations. The bricks were breaking up. Drivers worried that if their top speed in the flats went over 140 mph, accidents could become more serious due to track conditions.

As America began to pull out of the depression in the mid-1930s, Eddie Rickenbacker was determined to make the Brickyard safer. For the first time since 1909, major changes were made

to the track. The four turns were widened. New retaining walls and catch fences were built.

In 1937, Rickenbacker paved the four turns and the chutes with asphalt. The approaches to the turns were paved the next year. Infield fences were moved back, and more room was created on the inside of the corners.

By 1940, the only bricks in the Brickyard were on the front straight. They were left for sentimental reasons. But the Speedway itself had been transformed into a state-of-the-art paved oval. It was probably the safest track in the country.

As the Speedway became safer, rules were adjusted to allow cars to drive faster. In 1937 superchargers were allowed for the first time since 1929. The cars could run on high-octane

*The starter (on platform at left) waves the flag to begin the 1941 Indy 500. While the first race at the Speedway in 1911 had 40 entrants, the standard number of drivers is now 33.*

aviation fuel rather than the "dope" made of alcohol, benzol, acetone, and other volatile agents. The next year, the AAA adopted the European Grand Prix's formula for racing. This action opened Indy to European cars. Because Grand Prix cars ran on exotic fuels, racers were allowed to use whatever fuel they chose.

American financier Mike Boyle was attracted to the Italian Maserati racing car. He hired Indy car builder Cotton Henning to act as crew chief of his team and chose Wilbur Shaw as his driver. Then he ordered a custom Maserati from Italy.

Maserati engines, which ran at 6,500 rpm, were notorious for blowing up under the pounding of their long connecting rods. Crew chief Henning adjusted the gearing for Shaw's Maserati so that the engine wouldn't exceed 6,000 rpm. At that speed, the engine would run forever. Boyle's Maserati team won back-to-back Indys in 1939 and 1940.

In spite of the success of the Maserati, most teams stuck with classic dirt cars powered by Offy engines. They cost about $5,000, a fraction of the money Boyle poured into his Maserati.

By 1941, Eddie Rickenbacker had successfully solved the three problems that concerned him when he first bought the Speedway. Thanks to rule changes and improvements in both the track and cars, the minimum qualifying speed had increased from 90 mph to 115 mph. A wide variety of cars, including modified passenger cars, ran on the track. And the cost of racing successfully at the Speedway was within reach of most teams.

That same year, driving the Maserati, Wilbur Shaw almost won his third Indy in a row. But firemen putting out a blaze before the race washed off a chalk mark Shaw had placed on a faulty wheel. In the lead with only 120 miles to go, Shaw felt his right rear wheel tear loose. The car slammed into the wall. Shaw was rushed to the hospital. He later swore the suspect wheel was the one he'd marked. He promised to win the next year.

The next year's race never happened. By 1942, car racing was far from most people's minds. The United States was heavily involved in World War II. Most race car drivers and crew members were either serving in the military or working in factories that produced war materials. Gasoline, rubber, metal, and other car parts were needed for the war effort. The Indianapolis 500 was canceled for the duration of the war.

# TONY HULMAN'S REVOLUTION

W hen Wilbur Shaw returned to the Speedway in 1945, he could hardly believe his eyes. The track had remained padlocked and unused for more than four years, yet gaping cracks marked the asphalt turns. Grass grew between the bricks in the straightaway. The 37-year-old wooden grandstands looked ready to topple over with the next gust of wind.

Firestone, the tire manufacturer, had sent Shaw to Indianapolis to test a new synthetic rubber. As soon as he finished his tests, Shaw flew to New York to meet with Eddie Rickenbacker. The president of Eastern Airlines at the time, Rickenbacker was very busy. He told Shaw that he'd rather sell the Speedway than invest money in repairing it.

Wilbur Shaw was worried about the future of the Indy 500. Some of his finest moments as a race car driver had taken place at IMS. Over the next several weeks, he talked with many investors. Finally in September 1945, he presented the situation to Tony Hulman.

*Eddie Rickenbacker (center) signs papers selling the IMS to Tony Hulman (left) on November 14, 1945. Wilbur Shaw (seated right) became president and general manager of the Speedway, and T. E. Myers (standing) was appointed vice president.*

27

A millionaire with an avid interest in sports, Hulman agreed to take on the challenge. He'd grown up in Terre Haute, Indiana, and wanted the Indy 500 to continue. He was also a sharp businessman and recognized the potential for making big money. If the track failed, he could always sell the land to real estate developers.

On November 14, Tony Hulman bought the IMS for $750,000. He named Wilbur Shaw president and general manager of the organization. T. E. "Pop" Myers stayed on as vice president, bringing needed experience. The three men had less than six months to get the Speedway in shape for the 1946 Indy 500.

Carpenters reinforced seven of the eight grandstands. Grandstand G, built in 1915, was torn down. In its place stood a new, double-decked, steel-and-concrete grandstand. The brick and asphalt track was resurfaced.

While Hulman, Shaw, and Myers worked to get the Speedway in shape, racing teams faced their own challenges. The war was over, but car parts were in short supply. Car plants had been devoted to producing military vehicles during the war, so new car bodies didn't exist. The teams took prewar racing cars out of storage and did the best they could to get them in racing shape. It was close to impossible.

Memorial Day 1946 was sunny and hot. More than 150,000 fans heard Wilbur Shaw announce, "Gentlemen, start your engines." The command had been part of racing for decades, but over the next 10 years, Shaw made the call world famous.

Thirty-three cars started the race. Eighteen cars didn't make it through the first 250 miles. They literally began to fall apart. Only nine cars

were still running when the race ended.

Because of the challenges facing racing teams after the war, the AAA kept the prewar rules regarding what kinds of cars could be raced. The only significant change was to drop the weight restriction. This change allowed teams to use easily available dirt track cars at Indy.

The war brought important changes to racing, however. During the war, a number of innovations were made in airplane design. Many of these breakthroughs were then applied to racing cars. Features such as fuel injection, disc brakes, hydraulic shock absorbers, cast alloy wheels,

*A change in racing rules after World War II allowed dirt track cars, like the 1928 Ford shown here, to race at Indy. Keeping racers going was a challenge at the time because of the shortage of car parts.*

radial tires, and turbochargers were either invented or refined on World War II planes.

The war also brought many combat veterans to racing. Civilian life was pretty tame compared to bombing missions or frontline action. Driving race cars gave veterans a way to experience the intense excitement that came from combat. Many veterans who didn't actually race cars became avid fans of the sport.

Still, Tony Hulman wanted to draw more fans to car racing. His goal was to make the Indy 500 an integral part of Memorial Day celebrations. He continued to improve the Speedway, gradually replacing all the wooden grandstands and modernizing the Brickyard. He gave Indy the biggest purse in all of sports, ensuring that it would remain the most important car race in the world.

Hulman also had a vision for how the media could expand his audience. In 1949, live coverage of the entire race was broadcast over Indianapolis television station WFBM. This was not only the first TV broadcast of the Indy 500 but also the first television broadcast from Indianapolis.

As the popularity of the sport grew, Hulman and his associates decided to preserve the history of car racing. Many of the early drivers and innovators had died, and their accomplishments might have been forgotten. In 1952, the Hall of Fame was built at IMS to perpetuate "the names and memories of outstanding personalities in racing and the development of the automobile industry."

One of the developments still going strong at Indy was the Offy engine. Engineers made minor changes to the engine from year to year, but the Offy continually dominated the race. That didn't change when the next set of sweeping changes occurred.

In 1952, the Cummins Diesel Company asked Frank Kurtis to design a racing car that used a 401-cubic-inch Inline-6 engine, which was originally intended for heavy trucks. Kurtis faced a problem. The huge engine wouldn't fit in the car the way all other engines did at the time. Suddenly he had a great idea. He put the Cummins engine flat on the side of the car. The crankshaft went to the left, and the driveshaft went straight back to the rear axle. The driver sat on the floor next to the driveshaft.

Kurtis liked this approach so much that he built another car for millionaire Howard Keck. He called it the KK500A. This second car used an Offy engine, which was tipped 36 degrees to the right. The driver sat on the floor to the right, and the bodywork went right up around the driver's shoulders. Only his head was visible.

The first person who saw the car joked that it looked like the modified Model T used for amateur dirt track racing. Those cars were called "track roadsters." Soon the KK500A and other cars like it were commonly called "roadsters." They dominated Indy for the rest of the decade.

Other improvements also helped raise speeds at Indy during the '50s. After the 1955 race, the track was repaved. This provided better traction and removed most of the bumpy brick. Nylon-cord tires based on Firestone's World War II advances in aircraft tires were introduced. They were 1.5 inches wider than the older tires. Some teams began using fiberglass and magnesium for the car body, making it lighter and more fuel efficient. This reduced the number of pit stops.

Racing also faced problems. In 1954, Wilbur Shaw was killed in a plane accident. Tony Hulman became the new president of the IMS. Then in 1955, a series of fatal accidents within two weeks shook the racing world. On May 26, Formula One world champion Alberto Ascari was killed in Italy. Four days later, Bill Vukovich was killed at Indy.

As bad as those accidents were, they paled in comparison to the June 11 accident at Le Mans. As usual at that time, fans were standing near the pit. Nothing separated the pit area from the track.

Pierre Bouilion-Levegh lost control of his Mercedes-Benz 300SLR. It catapulted through the crowd lining the pit. His car exploded, sending fragments of glass and metal everywhere. At least 81 fans were killed. Hundreds were injured.

Overnight, car racing was perceived as a highly dangerous sport. People called for a ban on racing. The AAA, which had created rules for auto racing in America since the first decade of the 1900s, decided that racing was bad for its image. It ended its involvement in racing.

Tony Hulman was not about to close down the IMS. In the fall of that year, he organized the United States Auto Club (USAC) to take over the AAA's role in racing. He also made changes to the Speedway so that it would be safer for drivers, crews, and fans. By the 1957 race, a pit apron separated the pit from the track with a concrete wall.

Because Hulman approached racing as a business, he succeeded in making the Indy 500 highly competitive. It attracted top sponsors and huge crowds. Every race team needed at least one wealthy backer. With increased competition, costs were back up. To win the race, a

team needed at least $50,000. This was at a time when school teachers earned $3,500 a year and mechanical engineers at IBM had starting salaries of $5,200 a year.

By the end of the decade, Tony Hulman had revolutionized car racing. Car owners and sponsors worked with hired drivers and crew chiefs. They purchased parts from independent car builders, engine suppliers, and makers of exotic racing parts. That structure is still used today.

*Relatives of injured spectators search the debris of the 1955 explosion at Le Mans, France. In the aftermath of several fatal accidents, the AAA withdrew its involvement in auto racing.*

# THE GREATEST
# SPECTACLE IN RACING

The 1961 Indy 500 marked the 50th anniversary of the running of the first Indy. This Golden Jubilee race was surrounded by festivities honoring the anniversary, but the racing teams were more preoccupied with the appearance of a British Cooper-Climax.

What was so unusual about this car? While the roadsters that had dominated Indy during the 1950s had their engines mounted in front, the Cooper had its engine mounted behind the driver. It ran on gasoline rather than alcohol (like many race cars in those days), and the gas tanks were on either side of the driver. Even when modified to perform better on the Speedway, it weighed just 1,200 pounds, compared to the roadster's 1,600 pounds.

With its low profile and protruding tires, the Cooper reminded many people of a roller skate zipping around the track. Others simply called it "the funny car." The roadsters outperformed the Cooper on the straightaways, going about 160 mph, compared to the Cooper's 150 mph. But on the turns, the Cooper maintained 145 mph, while the roadsters

*A. J. Foyt (left) poses with Speedway president Tony Hulman after winning the 1961 Indy 500. Foyt would go on to win the famous race three more times.*

35

dropped to about 140 mph. Also, the Cooper got better tire wear and gas mileage, reducing the number of pit stops.

The 1961 race was tight. Seven different drivers held the lead. When the checkered flag waved, A. J. Foyt had won the race. It was the first of four Indy 500s he would win. The little Cooper finished in ninth. Its performance impressed many people. Its owners decided to adapt the Cooper's design.

First, Mickey Thompson tried to create a car that would keep the Cooper's advantages while adding more power. In 1962, he showed up at Indy with a mid-engine car featuring a Buick V-8 engine. Although Thompson's driver, Dan Gurney, had never raced at the Speedway, his qualifying time was good enough to put him in the third row. Problems with the car's rear end caused the Buick to drop out halfway through the race, but Dan Gurney wasn't about to give up on the idea.

He paid British car designer Colin Chapman of Lotus Limited to come to the 1962 Indy. Then the two men went to Dearborn, Michigan, to meet with Lee Iacocca and other executives at Ford. Iacocca was excited about the prospect of getting Ford involved in the Indy for the first time since 1935. When Chapman flew back to England, he had a contract to make three mid-engine cars for the next Indy.

Meanwhile, Ford produced a lightweight aluminum version of their 260-cubic-inch passenger car V-8. The Indy engine was a slightly smaller 255 cubic inches. It produced 376 horsepower (hp) at 7,200 rpm and weighed only 344 pounds.

In May 1963, Chapman arrived with the Lotus

*Jack Brabham wins the 1960 British Grand Prix in his Cooper-Climax, with an average speed of 108 mph. During the '60s, car designs —inspired by the Cooper's performance—led to increased speeds, and media coverage of racing intensified.*

29. It had a monocoque chassis. This style chassis eliminated the separate frame. Chapman made his monocoque racing cars from hollow boxes of aluminum sheet. They were held together with rivets. While the car looked flimsy, it provided more protection during an accident.

The Lotus 29 combined with the Ford V-8 weighed just 1,300 pounds. Two of the Lotus 29s ran in the race that year. Gurney started in 12th position and finished 7th. Jimmy Clark drove the other car and finished second behind Parnelli Jones. Jones's roadster leaked oil near the end of the race, causing Clark to slow his car so he wouldn't crash into the wall. Controversy

*The cover of Goodyear's spring 1999* Eagle Performance Report *featured A.J. Foyt and Indy winner Kenny Brack. During the 1960s Goodyear became an important supplier of racing tires; increased speeds were a direct result of improved tire technology.*

erupted when Jones wasn't black-flagged but pulled out of the race because of the hazard the leaking oil created. Even with Clark's car finishing just short of victory, it was clear that mid-engine design was the future at Indy.

The new car design created a need for new tires. The Lotus and its imitators were too small for the 18-inch rear and 16-inch front tires that Firestone had been providing for Indy since the early '50s. Firestone made special 15-inch tires for the Lotus in 1963. When roadster drivers tried the tires out, they discovered that the extra 1.5 inches that had been added to the width of the tires immediately increased speed by 3 mph.

There was one problem. Firestone only had enough tires and wheels for half the cars running in the 1963 Indy. Those teams that didn't get Firestone's 15-inch tires started listening to Goodyear's offers. Firestone lost its exclusive hold on Indy. During the next six years, tread widths increased from 6.5 inches to 12.0 inches. Aspect ratios (the ratio of the tire's sidewall to its tread width) dropped from 85 percent to 40 percent. And the tread compounds were much softer, giving better traction. Lap speeds went from 150 mph to 170 mph. Much of the increase was due to changes in tire technology.

Tires and car styles weren't the only things changing in racing during the 1960s. In 1964, Ford showed up at Indy with a four-cam V-8 engine. While that engine would soon dominate Indy, the 1964 race is remembered mostly for a terrible accident on the second lap. Dave McDonald, driving a Mickey Thompson–designed "skate," hit the inside wall of turn four. His full tank of gasoline exploded into flames. This set off a chain reaction. Eddie Sachs slammed into the flaming wreckage. His mid-engine Ford exploded. For the first time in history, an Indy 500 was stopped because of a crash.

When the smoke cleared and the wreckage was removed from the track, two drivers were dead. Eddie Sachs was killed instantly when his car exploded. Dave McDonald, his lungs burned, died a few hours later.

The race was restarted from the positions the

cars held at the time of the accident. When it was over, A. J. Foyt, driving a traditional roadster with an Offy engine, won again. After the race, A. J. talked about winning on a day when two drivers had died. "We are all sorry they died," he said. "That is racing. You can't let this get you down. . . . Maybe you haven't noticed it about me, but I haven't any close friends in racing. You can't let anyone get too close to you in this game. If they get killed, it breaks your heart, and if you are going to race, you got to race alone."

As a result of the 1964 crash, safety rules were tightened. The most important change was replacing fuel tanks with Firestone's variation of the fuel cell used in military helicopters. Inside a steel or aluminum box is a thick rubber bladder. Inside the bladder is plastic foam. If the metal box is ruptured, the bladder keeps the fuel from spilling. If the bladder is torn, the foam lessens the chance of the fuel spraying and exploding.

Other changes included increasing the minimum weight requirements and limiting fuel capacity to 75 gallons. The USAC banned pressurized fuel rigs. Gasoline was prohibited. Methanol became the standard fuel for Indy cars.

Everyone was thankful when the 1965 Indy race went off without a single accident. Two-time world champion Jimmy Clark won in his Lotus/Ford, followed by Parnelli Jones and rookie Mario Andretti. Only six roadsters were in the field. Mid-engine design was by then the norm. And Ford four-cam V-8s were also setting a standard. Seventeen of these engines were in the 1965 race. They placed first through fourth and were in eight of the top 10 cars. It was the first time since 1946 that the race had been won

by a car using something other than an Offy. The Ford repeated as winning engine in 1966 and 1967.

The 1966 race was again marred by a crash in the second lap, which stopped the race for an hour. While there were no deaths or serious injuries, 11 wrecked cars stretched across the track. Five other cars managed to wobble to the pits. When the race restarted, only 17 cars were

*Jimmy Clark celebrates his 1965 win at the Indy 500 with the traditional drink of milk (held by crew member, right).*

ready to go. Graham Hill became the first rookie to win the race since 1927, but the second serious accident in three races renewed calls for more safety measures.

Speeds increased even more with the 1967 introduction of turbine engines. "That's no racing car," said A. J. Foyt, describing Andy Granatelli's 2-foot-high, 12-foot-long, Day-Glo red torpedo, "it's a damn airplane."

Driven by Parnelli Jones, the car shot through qualifying laps at more than 166 mph. During the first 17 laps of the race, it broke one lap record after another. Suddenly, rain began falling. The race was stopped and for the first time held over until the next day. Only A.J. Foyt and Dan Gurney avoided being lapped by Granatelli's vehicle. Then Gurney pulled out with a burned piston.

With eight laps to go, Andy Granatelli stood in the pit, encouraging his car on. Famous for the bad luck that had stalked him at previous 500s, Granatelli thought this might be the year his team would finally win. It was not to be. A ball bearing failed in the gearbox, causing the car to break down.

Foyt took the mid-engine Coyote-Ford that he had made to the winner's circle. It was his third Indy win.

Over the next two years, the USAC reduced the allowable air inlet area until turbine engines couldn't be competitive. Turbocharged engines became the design of choice. But Andy Granatelli introduced other innovations that were copied by his competitors. One of the most important was the aerodynamic wedge shape.

Many people call the '60s the golden age of motor sports. When Ford pulled out of racing at the end of 1969, it had contributed to a radical change in how people approached racing. The Indy 500 had become the most expensive race in motor sports, and every year new ideas were tried. Drivers such as A. J. Foyt, Mario Andretti, Parnelli Jones, and Dan Gurney became household names with huge numbers of fans. But as had happened before at Indy, the high cost of racing was about to create its own problems.

# A Decade
# of Challenges

The 1970s presented a number of new challenges to the IMS. Televised coverage of all sports was exploding. More sporting events were competing for money from the same sponsors. Those dollars were needed to keep the Indy 500 in business.

Indy also could no longer count on the support of the Big Three American automakers. Ford, Chevy, and GM had no official presence at Indy during the '70s. Their engines were used in race cars, but the companies themselves were not directly involved. Instead they poured their money into creating more fuel-efficient passenger cars.

Competition in racing was increasing. Paved ovals and superspeedways replaced dangerous dirt tracks. Races at Ontario, Pocono, and Michigan joined Indy as part of the equation used to name the USAC's National Champion. The sport had to fight to keep its fans and drivers. Formula One races in Europe and NASCAR races were drawing a growing number of fans and attracted Indy teams and drivers.

As Tony Hulman looked over the situation with his keen business eye, he decided that the Speedway

*During the 1970s, new superspeedways such as Michigan's track (shown here) were built in an attempt to attract more fans to racing.*

45

would do more than survive. He would ensure that Indy remained the premier racing event. Having worked so hard to build up the Speedway, he had no intention of seeing its prestige slip away.

To meet his goal, Hulman took several steps. First, he poured money into projects that would increase the fans' enjoyment of Indy—building more entrances, grandstands, safety fences, garages, and hospitality suites. A new Hall of Fame Museum was erected, as well as a motel near the grounds. And a nine-hole golf course was renovated. The Speedway became a year-round destination for tourists, earning money throughout the seasons rather than only during the month of May.

Hulman also increased the size of the purse so the best drivers and teams would make sure Indy was part of their schedule. Having the best in the world participate would also guarantee plenty of media coverage and sponsorship. The total purse stood at a record $1 million in 1970 and swelled to $2 million by 1982. No other racing event came close to offering that much prize money.

Hulman's moves were successful. A crowd of about 260,000 spectators watched the 1971 Indy. The race was notable for two things: a new car design and four amazing occurrences. The new car was the McLaren M16. Based on the Lotus 72 used in Formula One racing, the M16 featured a wedge shape, side radiators, and no grille. It had two small spoiler wings in front and a large wing in the rear. Acting like upside down airplane wings, these spoilers pushed a car down toward the track, giving it better traction.

Using a longer wheelbase, the car's heavy

components were grouped in the center. With the help of a near-perfect suspension system, the M16 handled corners beautifully. Al Unser beat out the M16 for the victory, but the teams recognized the M16's potential. That year, McLaren opened a shop in Detroit to meet the demand for more M16s.

Unser's victory only took place after some amazing events. The first happened just as the race began. The pace car was pulling off the track when it swerved out of control and crashed into a photographer's stand. Twenty people ended up in area hospitals, but no one was killed.

The second happened moments later as Steve Krisiloff was speeding down the north chute. Suddenly, his Ford engine blew. Oil poured onto the track. Mel Kenyon's car slid into the liquid and crashed against a wall. Just as Kenyon was working his way out of the harness, he noticed

*Al Unser Sr. corners his Indy car. Unser won the 1971 Indy, which was also noted for four dramatic crashes.*

something out of the corner of his eye. A car was headed straight for him. "I dived right back into the cockpit," he recalled later. The other car slammed into Kenyon's wreck and vaulted over him. "[It] went right over my head," Kenyon said. "And I have the wheel marks on my helmet to prove it." When the third car landed, it crashed into Mario Andretti's vehicle. Pieces from four cars lay scattered over the track, but all four drivers walked away from the scene unharmed.

The third event happened on lap 113. Two cars smashed into each other on the main straight-away. The drivers were unharmed. Somehow, 24 other cars managed to work their way through the wreckage without another accident.

The final incident took place near the end of the race. Mike Mosley's car lost a wheel and spun across the track. Then it slammed into a broken-down car parked on the infield grass. The two cars exploded. Gary Bettenhausen, whose father had been killed at Indy in 1961, stopped his car to help pull Mosley out of the inferno. The driver was badly burned, but he survived. Winner Al Unser Sr. commented after the race, "We were lucky to win and lucky that no one was killed."

The combination of turbocharged engines and variations on the M16's "wings" increased speeds dramatically over the next two years. Throughout most of Indy racing history, speeds increased at about one mph per year. Between 1971 and 1973, however, lap speeds at Indy increased by 30 mph. Qualifying speeds exceeded 195 mph. Talk of breaking the 200-mph barrier grew.

Not everyone liked all this speed arriving so quickly. Winged cars were involved in many unexplained accidents. Critics complained that the speeds of the cars were more than the drivers could control. They argued that Indy should be a test of driving skill. When simply modifying a car's wing design could add 10 mph to its speed, some drivers had unfair advantages. What happened during the 1973 race strengthened those objections and led to major rule changes.

The start of the race was delayed four hours by rain. As the cars took off and swooped by the grandstand, David Walther's car jumped to the right. It hit another car and pinwheeled down the track. Flames and pieces of metal shot into a crowd of spectators behind a protective screen. Several cars crashed into Walther's vehicle. Walther was pulled out of his wreck badly burned, and more than a dozen spectators were injured, but there were no deaths.

The race was stopped to clear the track, but then rain delayed it for two days. Wednesday afternoon the race finally continued. After losing the lead during a pit stop, Swede Savage came streaking out, chasing Al Unser. As Savage headed into turn four, a rear wing tore off. The car crashed nosefirst into the wall. It skidded along the wall, flames enveloping it. As designed, Savage's uniform drenched itself with foam because of the high temperatures. This probably saved him from instant death.

An STP mechanic ran toward Savage's wrecked car but was hit by a truck and killed instantly. When Savage was pulled from the wreckage, both of his legs were broken. His eyes appeared to be glued shut. His hair was singed. Although conscious and talking during the ambulance ride to the hospital, Swede Savage died 32 days later.

The rule changes that followed included reducing the size of the fuel tanks from 75 gallons to 40.

*Janet Guthrie gets ready for the 1976 NASCAR Firecracker 400 race. The following year, she became the first woman to qualify and race in the Indy 500.*

The fuel had to be carried on the left side of the car, away from the walls of the Speedway. Cars could only use a total of 280 gallons of methanol, rather than 350. This change forced engineers to get better gas mileage, slowing the speeds of the turbocharged engines. Rear wingspreads were reduced from 64 inches to 43 inches, forcing the drivers to slow down on the turns.

The new rules were designed to make Indy safer. They succeeded. The 1974 race, won by Johnny Rutherford, was almost 10 mph slower, and the worst injury was a cut ankle.

Although the cars weren't using gasoline, the better mileage appeased some of Indy's critics, who saw racing as a waste of resources and a source of pollution during a time when fuel was in short supply and environmental concerns were increasing.

Other social issues impacted Indy during the '70s as well. In a decade known for many firsts for American women, Janet Guthrie became the first woman to drive at Indy. In 1976 she qualified for rookie tests. The next year, she became the first woman to qualify and race in the Indy 500.

The 1977 race was one of transitions. Ten months earlier, Tony Hulman had the entire oval repaved. The job was done with painstaking care. The oval was leveled. Then it was paved with a very fine, sticky asphalt and allowed to set for months before the trials. It was the last major project at the Speedway that Tony Hulman would oversee.

When A. J. Foyt won the 1977 race, becoming the first driver in history to win the Indy 500 four times, he asked Tony Hulman to ride in the pace car with him during his lap of honor. Five months later, Hulman died at the age of 76. Hulman's vision had guided the IMS for more than 30 years. His family would retain ownership of the Speedway, but for many racing fans, Tony Hulman's death marked the end of an era.

# THE FIGHT
# TO CONTROL INDY

Roger Penske has been a presence in Indy racing since the early 1960s, when he was a driver. By 1978, he'd built a personal fortune and one of the best racing teams ever—Penske Racing. With drivers such as Mario Andretti, Tom Sneva, and Rick Mears, Penske Racing was a serious power.

Like many owners, Penske felt the people financing racing should have more control over its rules. Along with 18 other owners, Penske founded an organization of Indy-car owners called Championship Auto Racing Teams or CART. Over time, CART began running the National Championship. USAC simply controlled the Indy 500. At first, most people were content with this arrangement, but it laid the groundwork for conflict that would shake Indy's foundations.

Such problems were far from most people's minds at the time, though. They were enjoying revolutionary changes in Indy cars. The 1979 race brought the first "ground-effect" cars to the Speedway, placing the driver between the front wheels. Behind him sat a

*Roger Penske, who started out as a driver, developed a winning racing team in the 1970s. He was one of the founders of Championship Auto Racing Teams (CART), which would later challenge USAC for control of the Indy 500.*

40-gallon fuel cell. Behind that were the engine and transaxle (a combination of the transmission and front axle). These and other modifications created a low-pressure area between the track and the bottom of the car, that "glued" the car to the asphalt.

Ground-effect cars became standard. Minor rule changes controlled the amount of downforce. They prohibited movable skirts and dictated a minimum distance between the track and the lowest point of the car. They also limited the size of wings and underwings. Good Indy cars still had about 3.0 to 4.0 g's of downforce. This meant that the force pushing an Indy car against the track was three to four times the car's weight.

Through other minor rule changes, the USAC and CART limited Indy cars to speeds of about 225 mph. They want to keep the sport safer and more interesting. By using similar cars, races focus on the drivers' skills, rather than on engineering feats.

A crop of popular drivers starring at the 500 and other Indy races brought more fans to the sport. Drivers such as Mario Andretti, Rick Mears, Al and Bobby Unser, Danny Sullivan, and Bobby Rahal had dramatic personal stories that added to their appeal. Rick Mears, for instance, won the Indy 500 in 1982 for the second time. Later that year, he crashed at the Montreal track and crushed his feet so badly that he almost lost them. Doctors told him he'd never walk again. After three months in a hospital bed, six months in a wheelchair, and countless hours of painful therapy, Mears came back. In 1985, he ran five races, and in 1988 he won his third Indy 500, posting the fastest lap ever at more than 220 mph.

Racing teams were excited by the addition of

*Rick Mears was one of many popular Indy drivers in the 1980s. After winning two Indy 500s, Mears had a serious accident in 1982. But he made a dramatic comeback and won his third Indy 500 in 1988.*

computers. Three onboard computer systems were introduced in 1985. First, ignition timing was taken off the crankshaft by a computer. This was more accurate than using a distributor. Second, the cars used electronic fuel-injection systems. Third, Indy cars used a "black box." This device stored and displayed information from up to 64 sensors throughout a car. Its data was downloaded into a computer during every pit stop. By the next pit stop, crews knew exactly what they needed to do to get the best performance from their car.

Expensive composite materials replaced

much of the cast iron and steel of older race cars. The chassis was mostly made of aircraft-quality aluminum honeycomb. The body was pure carbon fiber composite, known for being light and strong. Engines were almost completely aluminum. Magnesium wheels and titanium suspension arms were standard. By 1991, an Indy car cost about $300,000. That expense was about to trigger changes.

In 1989, Anton (Tony) H. George, the grandson of Tony Hulman, was named president of the IMS. Tony George held strong opinions about preserving his grandfather's legacy. He pushed for rule changes that would make Indy car racing less expensive. Car engines would once again more closely resemble those in passenger cars. George met a wall of resistance from the members of CART, who wanted Indy cars to be similar to the very expensive Formula One racing cars in Europe. Instead of holding races only at oval tracks, they wanted to include road races in the United States and in countries such as Brazil and Canada.

While this dispute simmered, CART teams rode under CART rules at most tracks but under USAC rules at Indy, which favored Tony George's vision. In 1994, Roger Penske and several other leaders in CART built a very expensive race car by making use of a loophole in USAC rules. While the car was legal, it represented everything the rules intended to keep out of the race. It easily defeated the rest of the field.

George and his supporters were angry. They changed the rules for the 1995 Indy 500 with only one goal: to keep Roger Penske's car out of the race. Penske modified his engine, but the car failed to qualify.

Shortly after the 1995 race, Tony George

announced plans for a new racing series. It would include the Indianapolis 500 as well as other races. Named the Pep Boys Indy Racing League, it is commonly called the IRL. The IRL was meant to be a direct challenge to the Indy car race series run by CART.

Though most members of CART were angered by George's action, a few, less wealthy racing teams joined the IRL. Tony George understood how hard it could be to finance Indy car racing. He went to great lengths to make it easy for IRL teams to get the money they needed, arranging lines of credit for them with Indiana banks. George also gave away free tickets to the races so there would be big crowds. He did everything he could think of to make sure the IRL racing series was a success.

In response, CART scheduled several of its important 1996 races on the same dates as IRL events. Tony George then said that 25 of the 33 spots at the 1996 Indy 500 would be reserved for teams that participated in IRL races. In December 1995, CART announced that its teams would boycott the 1996 Indianapolis 500. Instead, they would hold the U.S. 500 on the same day as Indy. It would be run at Roger Penske's Michigan International Speedway in Brooklyn, Michigan.

The IRL began its 1996 racing season under the last set of rules developed by the USAC, which became part of the IRL in 1997. The new rules cut the cost of an Indy car in half.

The conflict between CART and IRL continued. Many sponsors had to make hard choices. CART got commitments from Toyota, Honda, Ford, and Mercedes-Benz to build standardized engines for its cars, but some companies didn't want to

IMS president Tony George (second from left) hands out Indy 500 entry forms to a CART racing team in February 2000. A CART team had not raced in the Indy 500 since the IRL-CART feud began in 1995.

choose one Indy car group over another.

Valvoline had been supplying engine oil and fuel to the Indy 500 for 29 years. Its initial response to the conflict was to continue to sponsor both races. When each side demanded an exclusive contract, Valvoline broke off from both groups. Television coverage faced its own problems because of the conflict. ABC charged $200,000 for a 30-second commercial during Indy in 1995. In 1996, its ad rates were down to $160,000 for the same spot.

On May 26, the Indianapolis 500 started without the best-known drivers. A record $8.1 million in prize money was up for grabs, including $1.37 million for the winner. Buddy Lazier won the race by less than a second. Just nine weeks before, he had broken his back in 16 places. A special seat helped him make it through the race.

The CART-sponsored U.S. 500 did not begin well. A spectacular 12-car crash littered the track. This was particularly ironic because CART claimed to have the most experienced and safest drivers. The organization had made dire predictions about the results of letting inexperienced drivers compete at Indy. The winner of the CART event was Jimmy Vasser.

At the end of the day, there were no real winners. The Indy 500's audience on ABC was 20 percent lower than in 1995. CART's share of the audience on ESPN was one-third that of Indy. The conflict between IRL and CART continued throughout the '90s, but as the new century began there were signs of hope for Indy car racing. Important sponsors put pressure on the two sides to resolve their differences. Goodyear, for example, withdrew support from both CART and the IRL until the two sides stopped fighting.

CART and the IRL began to allow their teams to compete in each other's races. The IRL started to adopt some of CART's ideas for increasing the popularity of Indy car racing. The IRL is developing a road course at Indy for the first Formula One race to be held in America in decades. New partnerships with media groups such as Disney and its subsidiaries ABC and ESPN can make use of television and the Internet.

It's as if both sides are being forced back to Carl Fisher's original vision for the IMS. He wanted a huge facility that could be used to showcase many related competitions. He also saw the IMS as a place where tomorrow's technologies would be tested. He aggressively and creatively sought publicity through the media.

Indy car racing is at a crossroads. But the path forward still follows Carl Fisher's dream.

# GLOSSARY

| | |
|---|---|
| **Brickyard** | A nickname given to the Indianapolis Motor Speedway track. |
| **camshaft** | A long shaft that makes the engine's valves open and close. |
| **carburetor** | A device that supplies the engine with an explosive mixture of fuel and air. |
| **chassis** | The supporting frame of a car. |
| **combustion chamber** | The place in an engine where the fuel is burned. |
| **dope** | A fuel made of alcohol, benzol, acetone, and other explosive agents. |
| **downforce** | The force caused by air passing over and under a moving car that presses it down toward the ground. |
| **fuel cell** | A steel or aluminum box that contains a thick rubber bladder where fuel is stored more safely than in a tank. |
| **monocoque** | A car design in which the body and chassis are one unit. |
| **pace car** | A car that leads the racing cars once around the track before the race begins. |
| **pits** | Areas along the side of the track where cars refuel, change tires, and make repairs. |
| **pole position** | The place on the inside of the first row of cars at the beginning of a race. It's awarded to the car with the best qualifying time. |
| **spoilers** | Shaped like upside down airplane wings, these airfoils attached to the front and back of a car increase the amount of downforce. |
| **supercharger** | A device driven by gears or chains that produces more power and speed by forcing extra air and fuel into an engine. |
| **suspension** | The system of springs and other devices that support a race car on its axles. |
| **turbine engine** | Burning fuel in this engine spins a turbine, a series of curved fins mounted around a shaft. In cars, a mechanical connection takes power from the turbine directly to other moving parts. |
| **turbocharger** | A device driven by exhaust gases that produces more power and speed by forcing extra air and fuel into the engine. |

# CHRONOLOGY

1909    Indianapolis Motor Speedway (IMS) Corporation founded on February 8 by Carl Fisher; work begins on building track and facilities; first races held at the IMS.

1910    Surface is paved with bricks and the track is nicknamed the Brickyard.

1911    Ray Harroun wins the first Indy 500.

1913    Peugeot introduces overhead camshafts, wire wheels, and four-wheel brakes.

1915    Cars line up by qualifying speed for the first time.

1924    Fred Duesenberg brings the first supercharger to Indy.

1927    Eddie Rickenbacker buys the IMS.

1930    "Junk Formula" takes effect, cutting the cost of an Indy car from $15,000 to $1,500.

1935    Offy engine introduced; it powers the winning car and will dominate Indy for decades.

1936    Louie Meyer becomes first driver to win Indy three times; Rickenbacker begins major repairs and changes at the track.

1942–45    The IMS is closed during United States involvement in World War II.

1945    Tony Hulman buys the Speedway in November and begins major repairs.

1949    First live television coverage of the Indy 500.

1952    Hall of Fame built; Frank Kurtis introduces the roadster.

1955    A series of fatal accidents prompts the American Automobile Association (AAA) to end its involvement in racing; Tony Hulman founds the United States Automobile Club (USAC) to take over the AAA's role.

1961    Golden Jubilee race; Cooper-Climax introduces mid-engine concept.

1964    Another fatal crash at Indy leads to rule changes.

1967    Turbine engines appear for the first time; within two years, rule changes prevent them from being competitive.

1971    McLaren M16 introduces spoilers or "wings" to Indy.

1973    Another fatal accident at Indy; rule changes move fuel tanks to left side of car, reduce size to 40 gallons, and shrink size of wings.

1976    Janet Guthrie becomes the first woman to qualify for rookie tests; Tony Hulman has entire race course resurfaced.

1977    Janet Guthrie becomes the first woman to qualify and race in Indy 500; A. J. Foyt becomes first driver to win four Indy 500s; Tony Hulman dies.

1978    Roger Penske and others form Championship Auto Racing Teams (CART).

1979    Ground-effect cars make their first appearance at Indy 500.

1985    Computer systems used for the first time in cars, including "black box," which monitored data from as many as 64 sensors in a car.

1989    Tony George, grandson of Tony Hulman, is named president of IMS.

1995    Tony George announces formation of Pep Boys Indy Racing League (IRL), a direct competitor of CART races.

1996    U.S. 500 held at Michigan Speedway by CART on same day as Indy 500.

2000    The IRL announces that veteran CART drivers who want to race at the Indy 500 for the first time will not have to go through rookie tests.

# FURTHER READING

Andretti, Michael. *Michael Andretti at Indianapolis.* New York: Simon and Schuster, 1992.

Devaney, John, and Barbara Devaney. *The Indianapolis 500: A Complete Pictorial History.* New York: Rand McNally, 1976.

Dregin, Michael. *The Indianapolis 500.* Minneapolis: Capstone, 1994.

Friedman, Dave. *Indianapolis Racing Memories, 1961–1969.* Osceola, WI: Motorbooks International, 1997.

Shaffer, Rick. *CART: The First 20 Years, 1979–1998.* Center City, MN: Hazleton Publishing, 1999.

Stephenson, Sallie. *Race Cars.* Minneapolis: Capstone, 1991.

Taylor, Rich. *Indy: Seventy-five Years of Racing's Greatest Spectacle.* New York: St. Martin's Press, 1991.

# ABOUT THE AUTHORS

Bruce and Becky Durost Fish are freelance writers and editors who have worked on more than 100 books for children and young adults. They have degrees in history and literature and live in the high desert of Central Oregon.

PHOTO CREDITS:
NMI: 2, 9, 13, 19, 20, 29, 44, 47, 52, 55; Corbis/ Bettmann: 6, 33; International Feature Services: 14; Archive Photos: 16; AP/Wide World Photos: 23, 26, 34, 37, 41, 50; Goodyear/PRN: 38; Tom Strattman/Wagner Int'l Photo: 58.

# INDEX

Aitken, Johnny, 13
American Automobile Association
  (AAA), 10, 12, 24, 29, 32
Andretti, Mario, 40, 43, 48, 53, 54
Andrews, P. T., 8, 10
Ascari, Alberto, 32
Bouilion-Levegh, Pierre, 32
Bourque, William, 9
Boyle, Mike, 24
Championship Auto Racing Teams
  (CART), 53, 54, 56-59
Chapman, Colin, 36-37
Chevrolet, 45
Clark, Jimmy, 37, 38, 40
Cooper-Climax, 35, 36
Cummins engine, 31
DePalma, Ralph, 12
DePaolo, Peter, 15, 18
Duesenberg engine, 15, 18, 21
Firestone, 27, 31, 38-39, 40
Fisher, Carl, 7-8, 9, 10, 12, 15, 17, 59
Ford Motor Company, 18, 21, 36-39,
  40-41, 42-43, 45, 47, 57
Formula One, 32, 45, 46, 56, 59
Foyt, A. J., 36, 40, 42, 43, 51
General Motors, 18, 45
George, Anton (Tony) H., 56-57
Goodyear, 39, 59
Goux, Jules, 13-14
Gurney, Dan, 36, 37, 42, 43
Guthrie, Janet, 51
Hall of Fame, 30, 46
Harroun, Ray, 7, 11
Hill, Graham, 42
Hulman, Tony, 27-28, 30, 31-33,
  45-46, 51, 56
Iacocca, Lee, 36
Indianapolis 500, 7, 10-15, 18, 22,
  24-25, 27, 28-29, 30, 31, 32-33,
  35-43, 45, 46-51, 53, 58

Indianapolis Motor Speedway
  Corporation (IMS), 8, 10, 15, 17,
  27, 30, 32, 45, 51, 59
Jones, Parnelli, 36-37, 40, 42
Keck, Howard, 31
Kenyon, Mel, 47-48
KK500A, 31
Krisiloff, Steve, 47
Kurtis, Frank, 31
Lazier, Buddy, 58
Lotus, 36-39, 40, 46
Marmon Wasp, 7, 11
Maserati, 24-25
McDonald, Dave, 39
McLaren M16, 46-47, 48
Mears, Rick, 53, 54
Meyer, Louie, 21-22
Miller engine, 15, 18, 21, 22
Milton, Tommy, 15
Mosley, Mike, 48
Myers, T. E. "Pop," 28
Offy engine, 21-22, 24, 30-31, 40
Penske, Roger, 53, 56, 57
Pep Boys Indy Racing League
  (IRL), 57-59
Peugeot, 13
Rickenbacker, Eddie, 17-18,
  22-23, 24, 27
Sachs, Eddie, 39
Savage, Swede, 49
Shaw, Wilbur, 24-25, 27, 28, 31
Thompson, Mickey, 36, 39
United States Auto Club (USAC), 32,
  40, 42, 45, 53, 54, 56, 57
Unser, Al, 47, 48, 49, 54
Valvoline, 58
V-8 engine, 36-37, 39, 40
Vukovich, Bill, 32
Walther, David, 49